THIS BOOK IS BELONG TO

MISTAKES ARE PROOF THAT YOU ARE TRYING

YOU'RE BRAVER THAN YOU THINK

YOU ARE AMAZING

KEEP TRYING

NEVER GIVE UP

YOU ARE SPECIAL

READ KNOW LEARN

DREAM BIG

BE KIND

BE BRAVE

BE YOUR SELF

WE LEARN FROM MISTAKES

GREAT YOUR FUTURE

YOU ARE THE BEST

WORK HARD

BE CREATIVE

YOU ARE UNIQUE

YOU ARE SO CUTE

LEARN SOMETHING NEW EVERYDAY

SHOOT FOR THE MOON

YOU ARE SO CUTE

YOU ARE SO SWEET

WE LOVE YOU

ENJOY YOUR LIFE

THIS BOOK IS BELONG TO